SAUDI ARABIA EXPORT GUIDE

A GENERAL GUIDE TO SAUDI EXPORT RULES

MICHAEL O'KANE

ANDALUS PUBLISHING

ISBN: 978-1-945979-13-2 Print

ISBN: 978-1-945979-14-9 E-pub

Created with Vellum

CONTENTS

INTRODUCTION

The regulatory environment in Saudi Arabia is fast-moving. Regulations and directives are issued frequently and are not always widely available. While the trend today is to stay away from laws whose issuance was primarily cosmetic, there are still published regulations whose enforcement has been overtaken by technology or changes in Saudi society itself.

It was not that long ago, for example, that copies of all foreign newspapers sold in the country were physically reviewed by the Ministry of Information and advertisements that were deemed un-Islamic deleted or redacted with heavy black markets. With the decline in foreign newspaper sales this practice was abandoned. However, the law requiring approval from the same ministry for the importation of books and records remains on the books, even though sporadically enforced.

Saudi Arabia is a conservative society and products which offend Islam or the customs and traditions of the country will be prohibited or restricted. The Kingdom further insists that any product introduced into the Kingdom be safe; safely marked in the Arabic language and where there is any doubt, that the product be tested.

Despite the above, the Saudi Arabia is a mercantile society and the buying and selling of goods is consistent with the country's religious traditions. There is a long history of selling products from abroad and there is nothing in Saudi regulations which prohibits such importations, as long as the products imported are safe.

1

GENERAL

An importer must appoint an agent for the purpose of handling licensing and clearing goods in Saudi Arabia. The importer must be registered under the Ministry of Commerce. The importer must be licensed by MoC.

Saudi Arabia uses the Harmonized Commodity Description and Coding system for tariff classification purposes.

Distributors and Agents

Foreign companies usually appoint a distributor to handle sales of their products in the Kingdom. Companies may sell directly without a distributor but the entity created to do so must have at least 25% Saudi ownership. The required foreign investment license requires an investment of SAR 20 million ($USD 5.3 million).

The Manufacturing Alternative

A manufacturer may avoid the restrictions on local trading by manufacturing its products in-Kingdom.

2

DOCUMENTS GENERALLY REQUIRED

The following is a list of the minimum documents required to secure entry into Saudi Arabia. Products that require a special license or permission should also include those documents.

1. Commercial invoice
2. Certificate of origin
3. A clean ocean bill of lading or airway bill
4. insurance certificate
5. packing list
6. A copy of the consignee's Commercial Registration
7. A letter of authorization permitting the customs broker to clear the shipment.

THE INVOICE SHOULD CONTAIN the following information:

1. name of consignee (full info)

2. name of buyer (if different)
3. complete item description and material type
4. each item's unit price (no zero value)
5. unit weight and total weight in kg.
6. manufacturer name, address, country of origin
7. Harmonized System (HS) code for each item

A separate packing list must accompany each invoice, showing no value of the goods shipped.

These documents should all be:

1. Notarized by notary public
2. Certified by local country Chamber of Commerce
3. Certified by the Saudi Arabian Business Council
4. Legalized by Saudi Embassy or any Saudi consulate

All documents need to be translated into Arabic. Some documents may not be available in Arabic, such as bills of lading. At a minimum, the commercial invoice must be accurately translated.

These rules are subject to change.

3

TARIFFS AND TAXES

Saudi Arabia uses the Harmonized Commodity Description and Coding system for tariff classification purposes. A comprehensive list of Saudi Customs tariff schedule is searchable and can be found at https://www.customs.gov.sa/en/customsTariffSearch. Tariffs for particular products can be searched there.

Goods imported that compete with those produced domestically have a duty rate of 12 to 20 percent depending on the product. Dates, for example, are dutiable at 40 percent and cigarettes and other tobacco products are dutiable at 100 percent.

Certain goods are exempt from the external tariff. Goods manufactured and transported within the GCC states (Saudi Arabia, the UAE, Kuwait, Bahrain, Oman and Qatar) are exempt from duties. There are also a number of GCC-approved country-specific exceptions. Additionally, Saudi has a list of 758 exceptions that may be imported duty-free, including livestock and aircraft.

THE BOYCOTT IMPOSED on the State of Qatar resulted in the prohibition on the import or export of Qatari goods and services. There is also a long-standing boycott on Israeli goods, another boycott of Turkish products has from time to time been imposed as well. Sometimes informal boycotts arise due to current events which are later regularized in legislation; in other cases, when the offense is removed or apologies made the boycott is lifted.

SAUDI ARABIA GIVES preferential treatment to Morocco, Libya, Jordan and Tunisia, limiting customs duties on products imported from those countries to 10%.

Tax Rate:

Type	Customs Duty	Value-added Tax
Tax Rate Range	0% to 100%	15%
Customs Value*	CIF	CIF
Average Tax Rate	4.85%	5%
Tax Payer	Importers	Every member of the supply chain
Tax Collector	KSA Customs Authority	KSA Customs Authority
Customs threshold**	None	None

Value-Added Tax (VAT)

15% VAT is charged on goods shipped to Saudi Arabia. This amount is due at the time of customs clearance. As a GCC member, the VAT of 5 percent is levied on most goods imported from countries outside the GCC.

4

FREE TRADE AGREEMENTS

Saudi Arabia is a signatory to the Pan Arab Free Trade Agreement (PAFTA). This multinational treaty entered into force on January 1, 1988 and eliminated almost all trade barriers among its members by January 1, 2005.

There is a free trade agreement between the countries of the Gulf Cooperation Council and Singapore. There is an agreement between the GCC and the European Free Trade Area (EFTA); preferential treatment is also afforded to goods coming from Iceland, Norway, Switzerland and Liechtenstein.

If the product is manufactured in the GCC countries it will be entitled to duty-free entry.

Agreements and frameworks with other countries are being negotiated or developed.

5

TECHNICAL REGULATIONS

SASO has issued technical regulations for the following products:

1. Children's toys.
2. Low voltage Electrical Equipments and Appliances
3. Lubricating Oils
4. Detergents
5. Paints (Pigments) and Varnishes
6. Electrical Self-Balancing Boards (Scooter)
7. Building Materials - Part 1: The Sectors of Metals and their Alloys for Buildings and Constructions
8. Building Materials - Part 2: Insulation and Cladding Materials
9. Building Materials - Part 3: Hydraulic Bonding and Related Products
10. Building Materials - Part 4: Bricks, Tiles, Ceramics, Sanitaryware and Related Products

11. Building Materials - Part 5 : Tubes and Pipes used in water, electricity and Gas networks
12. Biodegradable Plastic Products
13. Gas Appliances and their Accessories
14. Truck Barriers
15. Electrical Lifts Used in Buildings and Facilities
16. Trailers and Semi-Trailers
17. Auto Spare Parts
18. Electrical Vehicles
19. Telecommunications Devices
20. Pressure Devices and Equipment and their Accessories
21. Games and devices of Amusement Parks
22. Jewelry Decorations and Accessories
23. Doors and Windows
24. Shoes and Leathers
25. Fireworks
26. Electrical Batteries
27. Packaging
28. Textile Products
29. Kitchen Tools and appliances
30. Tapes, Glue and Related Products
31. Fire Fighting Equipments and Materials
32. Personal protective equipment and clothing
33. Small Scale Solar PV Systems
34. Papers and Related Products
35. Machinery Safety - Part 1: Portable and Oriented Machines
36. Tires

37. Electronic Devices Used in Electronic Smoking Systems
38. Motorcycles
39. Tanks - Part 1 Tanks for the transport of petroleum products
40. Modified vehicles and limited production models

6

LABELING

The Saudi Arabian Standards Organization (SASO) has established rules for labeling and markings of imported products. Importers should strictly adhere to the requirements of SASO when importing products to the country to avoid the risk of rejection of products by the customs.

General Marking Requirements

Warning labels and safety instructions on the products should be written in Arabic (it also possible to write them in both Arabic and English languages).

For any other marking or labeling, one of the following methods shall be used:

1. Where the product falls under an applicable SASO standard, marking requirements shall follow the SASO standards. For example, SASO ISO 13006/2016 Clause 8.1- Tiles and/or their packaging should bear the marking in Arabic or in both Arabic and English in an

unremovable way (for instance carved or printed).

2. Where the product does not fall under any applicable SASO standard but falls under an applicable Regional/International Standard, the guidelines of the applicable standard, for instance, IEC/ISO/GSO/EN/ASTM standards, shall be followed.
3. Where the product has no applicable SASO standard, no applicable specific standard or no specific language requirements for marking, then the only guideline is that the marking language can be either in Arabic or English.

The essential characteristics shall be marked on the electrical equipment clearly and in a way that cannot be removed easily, or, if this is not possible, on an accompanying notice, and shall include the instructions for use, in order to ensure that electrical equipment will be used safely and in applications for which it was made.[1]

According to Gulf Standards, applicable to Saudi Arabia:

1. The Manufacturer shall affix the GCC Conformity Marking in accordance with the relevant Gulf Technical Regulations and requirements to each individual electrical equipment that is in

conformity with the requirements of the Gulf Technical Regulations in force.

2. The Manufacturer shall draw up a written Declaration of Conformity for each electrical equipment Model (Manufacturer Declaration of Conformity) in accordance with Article 17(1) and the model sets out in Annex (5), and shall keep it among the Technical Documentation at the disposal of the Competent National Authorities for 10 years after the product has been placed on the market. The Manufacturer Declaration of Conformity shall identify the product Model for which it has been drawn up.
3. A copy of the Manufacturer Declaration of Conformity shall be made available to the relevant authorities upon request. [2]

A copy of a Manufacturer's Declaration of Conformity template follows.

Annex (5)
Manufacturer Declaration of Conformity

Declaration of Conformity

Documents to be annexed with this declaration:

7

PACKAGING; PLASTIC BAGS

SASO requires that plastic packaging be biodegradable (M.A-156-16-03-03). Issued at the end of 2016, the regulation applies to all disposable products produced from polypropylene and polyethylene plastics. All plastic packaging, packing, and wrapping materials - including outer wrap for shipment as well as plastic inner wrapping used in imports of food (stretch-wrap and shrink wrap (stretch film) - are OXO degradable then bio-degradable.

The plastic products must be preregistered with SASO and apply the SASO logo before they are used as wrapping for imported products. Manufacturers of biodegradable plastic products must use additives licensed by SASO in manufacturing them. The additives used for biodegradable plastic products that come in contact with food should be safe for food according to relevant Saudi standards.

Special Cultural Rules

Importers should take care to comply with the following when drafting label contents:

1. Products should not bear any immodest or nude pictures;
2. Products should not bear a cross or pictures not consistent with Islamic morals;
3. The package should not bear Koranic or Islamic sayings;
4. Products and the packages should not bear photographs or illustrations of pigs;
5. If human figures are shown on packages, they should be in good taste;
6. Permission must be obtained for goods to bear the Saudi Arabian emblem, which consists of crossed swords and a palm;
7. Product information should be written in Arabic, or Arabic and English;
8. When writing production or expiry date, insert the day of the month first, followed by month and year.

8

CERTIFICATE OF ORIGIN

A certificate of origin is required for all commercial shipments to Saudi Arabia. The certificate of origin must be authenticated by a local chamber of commerce and should be translated into Arabic.

The Country of Origin marking shall be in the format "Made in xxx" or "Manufactured in xxx", in both Arabic and English languages. Any other format/text for marking the CoO is not acceptable.

Dual CoO marking such as: "Designed in xxx, Made in yyy" or "Assembled in xxx, Made in yyy" or "Engineered in xxx, Made in yyy" where xxx and yyy denote different countries of origin will not be accepted. It will only be accepted, if the name of the Manufacturer is clearly mentioned in the dual CoO marking text i.e. "Designed by [Insert Manufacturer's Name]in xxx,

Made in yyy" and likewise for the other two dual CoO variations (that is, "Assembled in," or "Engineered in.")

Certificates of Origin are verified through the FASEH platform. Under PAFTA, rules of origin require that the value added be not less than 40%.

If the product is too small to contain the Country of origin marking, then the marking shall be included in the packaging.

Samples for displays in shows or exhibitions are excluded from SASO's labeling and shelf life regulations but are subject to examination at time of entry.

9

CERTIFICATE OF COMPLIANCE

The Saudi Standards Organization issues Certificates of Compliance (CoC) to allow the importation of many types of consumer products. All imported goods must have a SASO Certificate of Compliance, issued by an authorized certification body in the country of origin or by SASO itself in Saudi Arabia.

Products without a SASO certificate will be refused entry by Saudi Port Customs or sent to the SASO to conduct a compliance test. If the test fails, the products will be refused entry, and all costs will be charged to the importing enterprise.

There are third-party lab-testing companies such as Intertek, QIMA, and SGS which can help importers and exporters with SASO certification.

Testing Required

SASO testing will be required in order to obtain a Certificate of Compliance. Machines must comply with the requirements of the Technical Regulations for Machine Safety issued by SASO. Article (4) of those regulations provide for consideration of basic health and safety requirements, technical requirements, instructions, metrological requirements, and requirements related to packaging.

Products must adhere to SASO's general energy efficiency regulations concerning air conditioners, washing machines, lighting products, electric motors, fuel economy for new vehicles, tires, clothes dryers, water heaters and the like.

10

SALEEM PRODUCT SAFETY STANDARDS

In January 2019, SASO introduced a new Saudi Product Safety Program called "SALEEM." The SALEEM program is designed to insures the safety of products imported to the Saudi market.

The SALEEM program is implemented via an online system called "SABER," a platform that enables manufacturers and importers to obtain the required Certificate of Conformity and Certificate of Shipment for consumer goods imported to the Kingdom of Saudi Arabia, upon registration in the system.

Currently, a number of technical regulations are being implemented for many categories of products. Products that are covered by a specific technical regulation, that is products that are are usually considered medium or high risk for consumers' safety, require specific conformity documents, such as test reports, risk assessment reports, and other documents, in order to obtain the Certificate of Conformity.

Conversely, for products not regulated by any technical regulation and which are generally considered low risk, a self-declaration that complies with the SASO guidelines is sufficient.

Once either the Certification of Conformity or the self-declaration is approved at the SABER platform, the importer can obtain the last document, i.e. the Certificate of Shipment, which allows the goods to enter the country.

11

SABER

The Saber online platform is a Saudi government-approved electronic services portal that helps the local supplier and factory to register the required conformity certificates electronically for consumer products, whether imported or locally manufactured, to enter the Saudi market. The platform also aims to restrict the introduction of unsafe products to the Saudi market.

The Saber E-Platform was developed under the supervision of the Saudi Organization for Standardization, Metrology, and Quality in cooperation with the THIQAH Business Services Company to operate and maintain the portal at a high level of efficiency and professionalism.

Entities that have registered on the SABER platform include[1]:

1. Ministry of Commerce and Investment
2. Saudi Standards, Metrology, and Quality Organization (SASO)
3. General Customs Authority
4. Conformity Assessment agencies

THE GOAL of the SABER platform is to reduce paperwork reduce paperwork and the time necessary to clear goods for entry into the Kingdom. The platform provides for the automated tracking of products and technical processes while monitoring the supply chain. Product Certificates of Conformity, required for the entry of goods into Saudi Arabia, can be registered on the platform.

12

MINISTERIAL RESPONSIBILITIES

No single Saudi ministry has comprehensive authority over importations. Books and other media containing information is the responsibility of the Ministry of Information. Medicines fall under the jurisdiction of the Saudi Food and Drug Authority. A non-exclusive list follows:

Books, Magazines	Ministry of Information (MoI)
Cards containing electronic information such as satellite TV cards, ID cards, maps	Ministry of Information
Chemicals	Ministry of Commerce and Investment
Compact Disks, DVDs	Ministry of Information
Computer Games	Ministry of Information
Cosmetics and Perfumes	Saudi Food and Drug Authority (SFDA)
Nutraceuticals	Saudi Food and Drug Authority (SFDA)
GPS Equipment	Communications and Information Technology Commission (CITC)
Ink Products, toner	Ministry of Commerce and Investment
Laboratory Chemicals and Solutions	Saudi Food and Drug Authority (SFDA)_
Medicines (prescription and non-prescription)	Saudi Food and Drug Authority
Photographic Media	Ministry of Information
Reagents and Diagnostics	Saudi Food and Drug Authority (SFDA)
Satellite Communication Equipment	Communications and Information Technology Commission (CITC)
Explosives	Ministry of Defense
Saudi Emblem, use of	Ministry of Information

13

PROHIBITED AND RESTRICTED ITEMS

Saudi Arabia has a few restrictions on what can be imported for religious and security reasons. It bans the import of alcohol, non-medical drugs, most non-Islamic religious materials and other materials deemed offensive. Goods such as weapons and electronic equipment are controlled for security reasons.

THE FOLLOWING IS a non-exclusive list of items whose entry into the Kingdom of Saudi Arabia is prohibited:

1. Alcoholic Beverages
2. Distilling Equipment
3. Animal blood products
4. Liquor
5. Narcotics
6. Poppy seeds
7. Loud or tune-playing car horns
8. Antiquities

9. Asbestos or asbestos-containing materials
10. Blank printed invoices for foreign companies
11. Christmas trees
12. Counterfeit products
13. Crosses, crucifixes, Stars of David
14. Dangerous, hazardous or chemical goods
15. Dogs without Saudi Embassy license
16. Firearms
17. Frog meat
18. Gambling devices
19. Laser pointers
20. Indecently packaged material
21. Musical greeting cards
22. Night vision binoculars
23. Nutmeg seeds and powder
24. Pork products
25. Pornography
26. Postal envelopes
27. Soil samples
28. Silk worms
29. Soil, leaves, stems, straw and manure
30. Tobacco advertising material
31. Used or retread tires
32. Electronic cigarettes
33. Personal metal detectors

Meat Products

Meat products require a "halal" certificate issued by an Islamic center in the country of origin to specify that the slaughtering procedures follow Saudi regulations. Specific permission is required for products such as agricultural seeds, live animals, books, chemical materials, pharmaceutical products, etc.

14

FOOD, COSMETICS, MEDICINES AND MEDICAL DEVICES

The Saudi Food and Drug Authority (SFDA) has jurisdiction over food and drug safety, monitoring standards for food safety including the use of pesticides in agriculture. Additionally, the agency acts to insure the quality of pharmaceuticals entering the country.

The following products require prior SFDA approval before receiving permission to enter the Kingdom. These products include:

1. Medications and pharmaceuticals (prescription and non-prescription)
2. Laboratory chemicals and solutions
3. Reagents and diagnostics
4. Nutraceuticals
5. Cosmetics and perfume

Private individuals may not import any items that require SFDA approval, including prescription medicine.

Cosmetics must be registered for importation on the FASEH and eCosma platforms.

Medical Devices

"The Saudi Food and Drug Authority (SFDA) regulates medical devices and IVDs sold and distributed in Saudi Arabia. For most devices, Medical Device Marketing Authorization (MDMA) approval from the SFDA is required before placing a product on the market. The SFDA meticulously reviews MDMA applications."[1]

To be approved in Saudi Arabia, a device must have already been approved in either Australia, Canada, Europe, Japan, or the United States. SFDA approval follows foreign approval.

A local Authorized Representative must be appointed if the device manufacturer has no local presence.

Submitting applications to the SFDA

Applications must include the following:

- Manufacturer and KSA Authorized Representative details
- Medical device information, such as intended use and labeling/instructions for use and all marketing materials
- Documents supporting market

authorization in the reference market (e.g., CE Certificate, 510(k) Letter, etc.)

- Proof of QMS compliance in your reference market
- Attestations that the device can withstand local environmental factors (e.g., extreme heat)
- Declaration of Compliance to Saudi regulations, and attestation of electrical compatibility if relevant.

SFDA approvals generally last for three years or are valid either for the remainder of the foreign approval if there is an explicit expiration date; or three years if foreign approval is deemed unlimited.

15

FASEH PLATFORM

The FASEH platform is operated by Saudi Customs and provides an online payment and other services, including even a truck-scheduling service to minimize waiting and reduce congestion.

The FASEH platform integrates the Saudi Post and Customs to speed clearance of packages sent through the mail.

The platform is also used to request Product Certificates of Conformity (PCOC) and Shipping Certificates of Conformity (SCOC) so that products may enter the Kingdom. Document expediters and customs brokers may submit commercial data and documents so that these certificates can be issued.

The Saudi government has outsourced testing of cosmetic products to private firms called "certifying bodies." There is no requirement that a manufacturer use one certifying body as opposed to another. The existence of a PCOC for a particular product will be registered with the SFDA. It is not clear what the SFDA would do if different certifying bodies reached different conclusions about a particular product.

The first step is submission of the product to a certifying body. The certifying body will test or obtain test results, collate other relevant data and information about the manufacturer and then register the product and this technical documentation on the FASEH platform, where it will be reviewed by the SFDA. If the SFDA is satisfied, the PCOC will issue. The SFDA has another platform called eCosma, where products are registered subsequent to their approval.

The following documents are necessary to clear products through customs ports:

1. PCOC
2. Bill of lading
3. Shipping Policy
4. Certificate of Origin and Customs Declaration
5. Commercial invoice
6. SCOC
7. E-Cosma registration

Changing Distributors

SFDA procedures provide for registering a new representative on the platform. If a manufacturer wants to appoint a new or additional distributors, a new distributor should open a new account on the eCosma platform and re-register all products there. Once this is accomplished the new distributor will be registered and can use the platform in respect of the products. All products previously registered must be re-registered.

The new distributor should be able to obtain PCOC's on his own without the cooperation of the previous distributor.

The following graphic shows the procedures for using the FASEH platform:

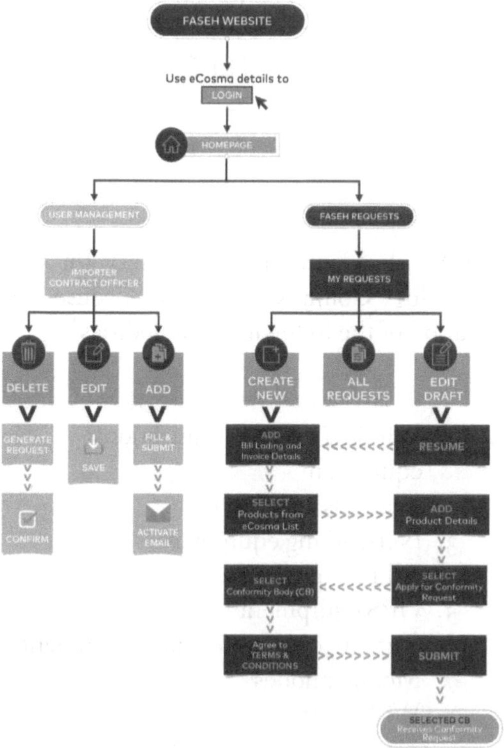
FASEH WEBSITE
Use eCosma details to
LOGIN
HOMEPAGE
USER MANAGEMENT
FASEH REQUESTS
IMPORTER CONTRACT OFFICER
MY REQUESTS
DELETE
EDIT
ADD
CREATE NEW
ALL REQUESTS
EDIT DRAFT
GENERATE REQUEST
SAVE
FILL & SUBMIT
CONFIRM
ACTIVATE EMAIL
ADD Bill Lading and Invoice Details
RESUME
SELECT Products from eCosma List
ADD Product Details
SELECT Conformity Body (CB)
SELECT Apply for Conformity Request
Agree to TERMS & CONDITIONS
SUBMIT
SELECTED CB Receives Conformity Request

16

COMPUTERS AND TELECOMMUNICATIONS

The Saudi Communications and Information Technology Commission (CITC) licenses the importation of the following commodities[1]:

1. Wireless telecommunications equipment
2. Wireless computers
3. Networking equipment
4. All IT equipment
5. GPS equipment
6. Satellite communication equipment
7. Mobile phones
8. Wi-Fi routers

Private individuals may import up to four items of personal use equipment. Five (5) or more items will be classed as a commercial importation and require CITC approval.

17

CHEMICALS

Chemicals, ink products and toner require approval from the Ministry of Commerce. The consignee must have permission to trade in chemicals or dangerous goods as part of its corporate objects; otherwise the Ministry will deny permission.

18

IECEE CERTIFICATION

An IECEE certificate (International Electrotechnical Commission System of Conformity Assessment Schemes for Electrotechnical Equipment and Components) is required for electrical equipment.[1]

Customers importing electrical and electromechanical equipment into Saudi Arabia require a Conformity Testing and Certification of Electro-Technical Equipment and Components (IECEE certificate), both issued by the Saudi Standards, Metrology and Quality Organization (SASO).

The electrical and electromechanical equipment include, but are not limited to:

1. Batteries (including mobile phone batteries)

2. Lighting equipment
3. Water pumps
4. Laptops and tablets
5. Washing machines and dishwashers
6. Televisions

Consignees in Saudi Arabia must apply for an IECEE certificate through the online portal at jeem1.saso.gov.sa, before the shipment is sent to Saudi Arabia.

ELECTRICAL PLUGS

Electrical Plugs

The regulations for electrical connections (plugs) are as follows:

Rated Voltage (Volt)127/220 +/-5 (domestic and commercial)

Frequency (Hertz)60 Hz. (+/- 0.1)

Plug typeG[1]

For more specific information, please see SASO 2203:2015, "Plugs and Socket-Outlets for Household and Similar Purposes-Safety Requirements and Test Methods 250 v/13 a."

Further technical information with respect to power cords and plugs is shown in the images below:

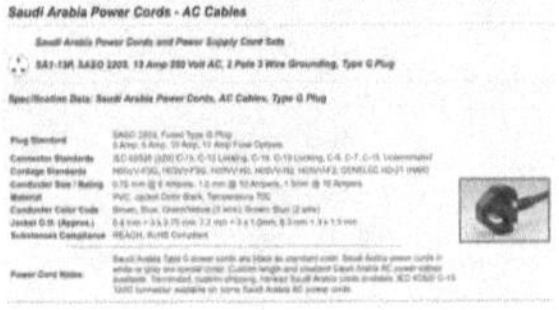

Saudi Arabia Power Cords - AC Cables

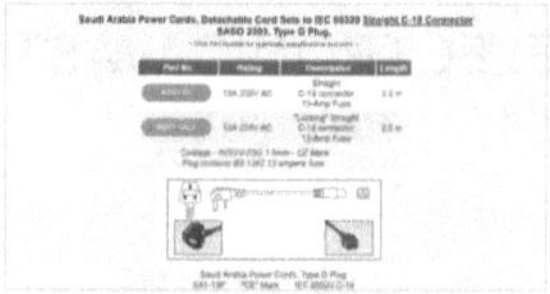

Special/ Other

Even though the Kingdom has standardized on 220v with British three-pronged outlets, there remain areas in the Kingdom (such as Saudi Aramco) where power is supplied at 110v with American flat plug outlets.

20

ELECTRONIC WASTE

The Chemical Safety and Hazardous Wastes department at the General Authority of Meteorology and Environment Protection is responsible for taking care of E-waste management in Saudi Arabia.

IN SAUDI ARABIA, waste management environmental regulations are mainly intended to manage municipal and industrial hazardous and non- hazardous solid waste. As of 2018, there were no specific requirements in the regulations that govern the management of e-waste.

EVEN THOUGH THERE are no clear regulations on e-waste management in Saudi Arabia, but the country is starting to realize the need to adopt a sustainable e-waste management approach. The major challenges are that there is no proper method for e-waste handling (collection and transporting) and there is a very low public awareness about e-waste recycling[1].

21

PACKAGING AND LABELING

Arabic and English should be used for all of these package inserts or labels. If a warranty card is included, it should be in Arabic, or Arabic and English.

Please see the above section on "Packaging and Labeling."

Additionally, the following information should be contained in the product packaging:

1. Producer's name and address;
2. Production and expiration dates in Arabic and English languages

Safety and instructional manuals must be supplied in the Arabic language or Arabic and English.

. . .

Warning instructions are mandatory. Warning labels must be difficult to remove.

22

FIBER CONTENTS

The contents and composition of textile products must stated. The languages used to communicate this information are Arabic and English. A "Country of Origin" certificate is required. Product care information is required and should be communicated to the consumer in Arabic and English. For manufactured clothing, size information in Arabic and English is required.[1]

The technical regulations for textile products is found at SASO Article3/2/2 ⁋ (F) requiring that each multi-fiber textile product must contain the data on all of its component fibers and their percentage by weight in descending order and the relevant standard specifications shall be determined to determine the percentages of the component fibers, taking into account a tolerance of 5% of the percentages of major fibers mentioned in the explanatory data.When it is not possible to easily identify some fibers during manufacturing, the term "Other Fibers" can be added, followed by a percentage by weight, in the following two cases:

1. When the fiber is of one type and does not exceed 5% of the total weight of the textile product.
2. When the fibers are mixed and their total does not exceed 15% of the total weight of the textile product.

Technical information that must be included on the product's data card:

1. With regard to fibers: add the descriptions of the fibers presented in the market, and tightly labeled on the packaging medium,
2. For sewing thread packages: the thread number is added, and the card is added to each spool,
3. Concerning fabrics: fixing the tag on the packaging medium, and on a part of the roll permanently, so that the card remains attached and visible in the shops.
4. For clothes: the card is attached or sewn tightly to the dress, and the coding data for the sizes of the clothes are added according to the relevant standard,

5. For carpets and rugs: Technical characteristics and terms of use shall be added, and the information must appear on the card that is firmly affixed or affixed to the back of the product.

23

PLASTIC PRODUCTS

All poly bags with an opening of 12.7cm or larger must have a "suffocation warning." Example: "Plastic bags can be dangerous. To avoid danger of suffocation; keep this bag away from babies and children." This warning must be given in Arabic and English.

Plastic products must meet the requirements of the technical regulation for degradable plastic products, for example (that the supplier has a commercial register, that the product has completed the conformity assessment procedures, the product has an effective environmental management system or has ISO 14001 certification, accompanied by a Certificate of Conformity which must be submitted by the supplier, along with a a laboratory report showing that only licensed and safe materials have been used and that the information used in placing the degradable plastic logo is correct and established, and the data card supplied with the product matches the Saudi standard specifications.

Imports Checked at Customs

Products and packaging made with polyethylene or polypropylene must comply with the new rules and contain an oxo-biodegradable masterbatch from a supplier approved by the Saudi Arabian government. In order to check imported products accurately, Saudi Customs works with independent laboratories.

Which products are affected?

As of December 12, 2017, the plastic products (which are listed on the HS code list) and the packaging materials for the consignments must gradually bear the "biodegradable" logo. This applies to disposable plastic products made of polyethylene or polypropylene with a film thickness of 250 microns or less, which are commonly used for packaging (such as carrier bags, wrappings and similar applications), are oxo-biodegradable. Without the corresponding logo, the exports cannot be imported into Saudi Arabia. In order to use the logo, the importers and manufacturers need a license from the responsible organization SASO. At the same time, the companies must attach a letter of commitment from the importer, stating that the regulations for biodegradable plastic products will also be followed for future shipments.

An example of such required logos is shown below.

Care Instructions

Instructions for the care and operation of the product must be provided in the Arabic language or Arabic and English.

24

ADDITIONAL REGULATORY REQUIREMENTS

Products that can be classified as children's toys[1], must be accompanied by instructions and safety instructions in the Arabic language. If the "manufacturer considers, or has evidence of suspicion, that the products he has placed on the market do not conform to the applicable Gulf technical regulations, he must immediately notify the corrective actions necessary to make those products conform, and withdraw or recall them if necessary."

25

WARRANTY/ GUARANTEE

Under consumer law in the Kingdom of Saudi Arabia, consumers are entitled to a free of charge repair of defective goods and if the defect is re-occurring, a replacement of the goods. These rights expire two years from date of purchase. The warranty is extended for a one-year period if there has been delay in providing spare parts or after maintenance during the warranty period. The responsibility to provide a remedy is on the seller, the agent and/or the manufacturer of the product.

In 2014, the Ministry of Commerce issued a new "know your rights" statement in which it announced that all electric appliances, vehicles and electronics are to have at least a minimum of two years warranty.

Contractual Warranty/Guarantee

. . .

A CONTRACTUAL GUARANTEE beyond the required two years must be in Arabic and English as this is the rule for all instruction manuals.

THE LENGTH of the contractual warranty may not be limited to one year as this is less than the mandatory two-year period and the recovery is in any case the same.

26

COMMUNICATIONS WITH CUSTOMERS

Hotline/Phone Number

There is no hotline or phone line requirement. However, the distributor of the products must "establish a clear procedural mechanism to settle consumer complaints without fees that includes responding quickly to the complaint with information and procedures for submitting the complaint."[1]

A recent regulation by the CITC requires call centers that service Saudi customers to be located in Saudi Arabia. This is an outgrowth of the new Personal Data Protection Law; regulations implementing that law are to be issued before the law takes effect on March 24, 2022.

Importers must create a product complaints registry.

27

INTELLECTUAL PROPERTY

Trademarks

A company that seeks to protect its mark in Saudi Arabia should register that mark. Registration in another country does not necessarily afford protection in Saudi Arabia. A product that is manufactured abroad and carries the ® symbol will not necessarily be denied entrance due to the use of a trademark registered in a foreign country.

As a practical matter, trademarks must be registered in order to display the mark on signage at local business locations. To register the trademark, a copy of the license agreement and proof of registration of the trademark are required before the Saudi municipality agency (the *Baladia*) will issue permission to display signage.

The Saudi Authority for Intellectual Property is the agency tasked with registering trademarks. The GCC Trademark Law was approved by the Kingdom in 2014.[1] Implementing regulations entered into force on September 27, 2016.

For the registration of a mark, Saudi Arabia has adopted the international Nice Classification in accordance with the Agreement Concerning the International Classification of Goods and Services for the Purposes of the Registration of Marks of 1957. Proof of use is not required for registration or renewal. Registration only applies to Saudi Arabia.

Saudi Arabia is a member of the Paris Convention and accepts priorities from Convention application. Saudi Arabia grants a right of priority to applications filed in Convention states within a period of six months post-filing. Substantial similarity of a priority application with the application filed in Saudi Arabia and within the same class is a condition of claiming priority. Minor amendment in later trademarks are allowed. Collective or certification marks are recognized.

Duration of the registration is for ten Hejira years. Renewal must be filed within the last year of registration. There is a six-month grace period prior to cancellation.

A trademark application must contain the following information:

1. An image of the mark and an accurate description.
2. The goods or services covered by the trademark.
3. The priority application date, number and state in which it has been filed, if any.
4. A power of attorney, properly

legalized, if the application is submitted by an agent.

5. If the trademark contains a word in a foreign language, a translation into Arabic.
6. For local companies, a copy of that company's Commercial Registration Certificate.

Saudi Arabia's 2002 Trademarks Law[2] brought Saudi Arabia's trademarks regime into compliance with the provisions of the TRIPS Agreement. The Trademarks Law superseded all earlier laws on trademarks. The Implementing Regulations[3] for that law date from the same year.

The main features of the new Trademarks Law and implementing regulations are:

1. Increase and impose harsher punishments, with the maximum of SAR 1,000,000;
2. The right of the injured party to compensation in proportion to the damages suffered by the injured party due to infringement;
3. The right of the injured party to obtain an attachment order;

Third parties are given standing to file a complaint against the granting of trademark registration. Well-known trademarks are protected, even if not registered. Trademarks covering alcoholic goods may not be registered. Once a trademark or a service mark application is filed, it is examined as to its availability, registrability, and coverage. If the Registrar objects in writing to certain aspects of the mark in the course of examination, such as the scope of goods or services or asks for modification of the mark, a grace period of 3 months is given to the applicant concerned to comply with the Registrar's request.

Once the application is formally rejected, a complaint against the rejection can be filed before the Oppositions and Complaints Committee within 30 days from the date of notification of the rejection. The decision of the Committee may be appealed before the Minister of Commerce and Minister's decision may be appealed to the Board of Grievances. The trademark or service mark applications accepted for registration by the Registrar are published in the Official Gazette of Saudi Arabia.

Publication is an invitation to any interested party to oppose the registration of trademarks or service marks conflicting with their interests. There is a three-month period open for filing opposition by any interested party. An opposition to the registration of a trademark or service mark should be filed within the term of the opposition period, i.e., 90 days from the date of publication of the notice in the Official Gazette. The case is referred to the Oppositions and Complaints Committee and, if the decision is not satisfactory to either party, they may file an appeal within 30 days to the Board of Grievances.

The duration of a trademark or a service mark registration is for 10 years from the filing date according to the Hijri (Islamic) calendar (equivalent to approximately 9 years and 8 months). The registration is renewable for similar periods of 10 years each. No grace period is allowed for filing a renewal application. However, a fresh trademark application can be filed for the re-registration of a cancelled trademark or service mark.

A trademark can be licensed, pledged or transferred by the rightful owner. The trademark may be deleted or cancelled if it is not used for five consecutive years. Penalties for infringement of a valid trademark include imprisonment for a period of not more than one year and a fine of not less than SR50,000 and not more than SR1,000,000. Any civil or criminal disputes arising from the infringement are reviewed by the Board of Grievances.

If the importer of a product is also the licensed trademark owner, he can prohibit the import of the products by others as violating his trademark. This can be an issue when a foreign company seeks to replace its distributor or add additional distributors.

Patents

Saudi patent protection is granted for twenty years from the date the application is filed. Saudi Arabia is a signatory to the Patent Cooperation Treaty. A unitary patent application may be filed to achieve protection throughout the GCC.

There are two overlapping patent registration systems in Saudi Arabia. A regional law, the

GCC Patents of Inventions Regulation of 2001[4] permits the registration of patents with effect throughout the GCC countries. The GCC Patent Office is based in Riyadh.

Otherwise, patents are governed by the Layout Designs of Integrated Circuits, Plant Varieties, and Industrial Models Regulation[5] which gives effect to the Paris Convention for the Protection of Industrial Property.

A protection document is granted by the General Directorate of Patents at King Abdulaziz City for Science and Technology, which gives full protection within the Kingdom to an invention, a layout design of an integrated circuit, a plant variety, or an industrial design. The protection document grants the owner the right to commercially exploit the subject matter of protection.

Protection is granted to the owner for a duration of 20 years for an invention, 10 years for an industrial design and a layout design of an integrated circuit, and 20 to 25 years for a new plant variety. The above periods are renewable, for an annual fee.

Registered Designs

Designs and industrial models in Saudi Arabia are governed by Patents, Layout Designs of Integrated Circuits, Plant Varieties and Industrial Models Law[6] which provides full protection for patents, layout designs of integrated circuits, plant varieties and industrial designs in Saudi Arabia entered into force in 2004. Absolute universal novelty is stipulated by the design law.

However, applications are examined as to formalities only. Protection period for industrial designs and models is 10 years from the date of filing the application.

Confidential Information

Saudi Arabia has several laws which protect confidential information.

Saudi Arabia is a member of the World Trade Organization, which requires its member nations to implement laws protecting intellectual property and trade secrets [the TRIPS Agreement]. Consequently, the Kingdom of Saudi Arabia adopted its Regulations for the Protection of Trade Secrets Information[7] which provide a remedy for unauthorized disclosure of commercial secrets when done in a manner contrary to honest commercial practices.

The Ministry of Commerce and Industry issued Implementing Regulations[8] providing for protection of undisclosed test and other data. Saudi Arabia would protect such data against disclosure, except where necessary to protect the public, or unless steps were taken to ensure that the data were protected against unfair commercial use. Any person harmed as a result of violations of the provisions of the Law may file a lawsuit to claim compensation for damages sustained.

Saudi Arabia has several other laws which contain provisions protecting confidential information or trade secrets such as the Companies Law, Labor Law, Banks Control Law and the procedural rules of the Communications and Information Technology Commission.

Websites

Saudi Arabia does not censor manufacturer's websites in another country unless such site contains material which is offensive to Islam or the customs and traditions of the Kingdom. If found to be objectionable, the Kingdom will make such websites unreachable from within national territory.

28

CUSTOMS BROKERS AND FREIGHT FORWARDERS

The following is a non-exclusive list of companies in Saudi Arabia which provide brokerage services.

Crown International

Crown International is a freight forwarding and logistics company based in Dammam, Saudi Arabia with branches in Jeddah and Riyadh. The company has affiliate offices in Hyderabad, Delhi India and Dubai.

Crown International accepts freight such as textiles, toys, machinery, handicrafts, food and beverages, cosmetics, furniture, and electronics.

Freight Services:

•Ocean Freight (FCL): Yes

•Ocean Freight (LCL): Yes

•Inland Truck Freight: Yes

•Air Freight: Yes

•Custom Clearance: No

•Insurance: Yes

•Warehousing: No

Company Overview
•Founded: 2011
•HQ: Riyadh, Kingdom of Saudi Arabia

Natco Middle East

Natco Middle East was established in 2017 in Jeddah, Saudi Arabia. The company has branch offices in Riyadh, Dammam, and Dubai.

Natco's services include ocean and air freight, land transportation, customs clearance, warehousing, and distribution.

Freight Services
•Ocean Freight (FCL): Yes
•Ocean Freight (LCL): Yes
•Inland Truck Freight: Yes
•Air Freight: Yes
•Custom Clearance: Yes
•Insurance: Yes
•Warehousing: Yes
Company Overview
•Founded: 2017
•HQ: Jeddah

Uniworld

Uniworld Freight Services offers a comprehensive range of shipping and add-value services, including ocean, air, inland transportation, warehousing, and customs clearance.

Freight Services
•Ocean Freight (FCL): Yes
•Ocean Freight (LCL): Yes
•Inland Truck Freight: Yes

•Air Freight: Yes
•Custom Clearance: Yes
•Insurance: No
•Warehousing: Yes
Company Overview
•Founded: 2003
•HQ: Jeddah

Gulf System

GFS specializes in the air and sea freight forwarding.Their services include customs service, international freight forwarding, door to door express service, domestic transportation, warehousing, and distribution.

Freight Services
•Ocean Freight (FCL): Yes
•Ocean Freight (LCL): Yes
•Inland Truck Freight: Yes
•Air Freight: Yes
•Custom Clearance: Yes
•Insurance: No
•Warehousing: Yes
Company Overview
•Founded: 2003
•HQ: Riyadh

Speed Trans Logistics

Speed Trans Logistics provides end-to-end design, implementation and operational capabilities in freight forwarding, contract logistics, transportation, and distribution management.

The company optimizes clients' overall

supply chain by providing integrating multiple logistics functions starting from material and product collection, warehousing, value-added services, distribution and cross-docking.

Freight Service

- Ocean Freight (FCL): Yes
- Ocean Freight (LCL): Yes
- Inland Truck Freight: Yes
- Air Freight: Yes
- Custom Clearance: Yes
- Insurance: No
- Warehousing: Yes

Company Overview

- Founded: 2015
- HQ: Jeddah, Kingdom of Saudi Arabia

NOTES

6. Labeling

1. Gulf Technical Organization Standards, Annex 1
2. Annex 3, 3(a)

11. Saber

1. (Source: https://saber.sa/home/aboutsaber)

14. Food, Cosmetics, Medicines and Medical Devices

1. Source: https://www.emergobyul.com/services/saudi-arabia/saudi-arabia-registration. Emergo specializes in obtaining approval for medical devices and acting as a Saudi in-country manufacturer's representative.

16. Computers and Telecommunications

1. The CITC publishes a full list of items whose importation must be licensed at https://bit.ly/3qslucq.

18. IECEE Certification

1. (Source: https://www.customs.gov.sa/en/general/import-instructions)

19. Electrical Plugs

1. Source: GCC Standardization Organization, Gulf Technical Regulation

for Low Voltage Electrical Equipment and Appliances BD-1420XX-01, (1 July 2016)

20. Electronic Waste

1. Alameer, H. (2015) Integrated Framework for modelling the Management of Electronic Waste in Saudi Arabia. [Online] Available from: http://vuir.vu.edu.au/32316/1/ALAMEER%20Hasan %20-%20Thesis.pdf.

22. Fiber Contents

1. Source, US Dept of Commerce, Int'l Trade Administration, Office of Textiles and Apparel, https://otexa.trade.gov/labeling.pdf

24. Additional Regulatory Requirements

1. SASO Technical Regulation for Children's Toys, Article 4 ⁋9.:

26. Communications with Customers

1. Article (25) of the "Rules for the Provision of Maintenance and Provision of Spare Parts"

27. Intellectual Property

1. Royal Decree No. 51, dated 25 May 2014.
2. Royal Decree M/21 of 29/5/1423H (7 August 2002)
3. Ministerial Order No. 1723 dated 4 October 2002.
4. Royal Decree No. M/28 of 2001
5. Royal Decree No. M/27 of 20/5/1425 H (17th July 2005)
6. Royal Decree No. M/27 dated July 17, 2004
7. Council of Ministers Resolution No. 50, dated 25/2/1426 H (April 5, 2005).
8. Ministerial Decision No. 3218 of 25/3/1426H (4 May 2005), as amended by Ministerial Decision No. 431 of 1/5/1426H (8 June 2005).

ABOUT THE AUTHOR

Michael O'Kane is an attorney with fifteen years' experience in Saudi Arabia and the Middle East. He is a former special legal advisor to the Kingdom of Saudi Arabia and in that capacity drafted a legal code, including a disputes resolution code, for the Kingdom's Economic Cities project. He advised the Saudi Railways Commission and assisted them in drafting regulations. He advised KA-CARE, the King Abdullah City for Atomic and Renewable Energy in drafting a law for the peaceful use of nuclear energy in the Kingdom. His book, *Doing Business in Saudi Arabia* is on Amazon's International Law bestseller list. He is the author is *Doing Business in Saudi Arabia, Saudi Securities Law, Saudi Labor Law Outline; Saudi Real Estate Law* and *Law and Rockets: An American Lawyer in Iraq*. He is rumored to be the author of *Don't Forget to Tape the Toilets: The Missing Employee Orientation Manual for Saudi Arabia and Bahrain.*

He may be contacted at mok@mu7ami.com.

Business & Economics/Exports & Imports

The proliferation of agency platforms has complicated, rather than simplified, the process of qualifying goods for importation into Saudi Arabia.

This handbook digests the applicable rules and guides the exporter through the complicated process of shipping goods to the Kingdom.

The author has worked for many years as an attorney in the Kingdom, both in the private sector and as an advisor to the Saudi government.

ISBN 978-1-945979-13-2

9 781945 979132 >

ANDALUS
PUBLISHING